California
Wildflowers

A children's field guide to the state's most common flowers

Interpreting the Great Outdoors

Illustrations by DD Dowden, text by Beverly Magley

To Mom and Dad,
with love,

dd

Publishers: Michael S. Sample, Bill Schneider
Editor: Christopher Cauble
Design, illustration, and typesetting: DD Dowden.
Botanical consultant: Christopher Hobbs

Design, illustrations, typesetting, and other prepress work by Falcon Press, Helena, Montana. Printed in Singapore.

Library of Congress Number 88-83883
ISBN 0-937959-58-8

Contents

Introduction

Zing! The brilliant yellow and deep red colors of a wildflower grab your attention. On bent knee to look more closely, you sniff the lovely fragrance and admire the beauty. While there, it's easy to notice more flowers, tiny and shy, tucked close to the earth. Shiny green leaves have many shapes and sizes, and the world of flowering plants becomes more interesting. Some are just poking up through the ground, others have tightly furled buds not yet ready to open, still others are in full bloom.

Lie on your back and look at a flower as it splashes its color up to the sky. Turn onto your side and get an ant's-eye view of the world. Then go belly-down to see how many different plants are growing right under your nose. It's amazing!

California wildflowers grow in many different types of habitats—from the lowest, hottest, driest spot in the United States to the rain-soaked redwood forests along the coast to the alpine highlands of the Sierra Nevada. You can find pleasure in the many wildflowers by watching them grow and blossom. At last count, botanists identified 7,000 different wildflowers in California.

Flowers have common names, like our nicknames, that often tell something about them. Fairy slipper, tiger lily, or shooting stars are descriptive names. But these names can be confusing because many flowers have several common names. If you get confused, learn the scientific names. Once you know some of the main features of a flower family, it becomes easier to name individual members of that family.

Wildflowers usually wilt rapidly, even if you rush them into a vase. Enjoy, study, and get to know them, but leave them to grow and delight the next person. After all, wildflowers always look better in their own home than in ours.

I will be the gladdest thing under the sun!
I will touch a hundred flowers and not pick one.

Edna St. Vincent Millay,
"Afternoon on a Hill"

Redwood Forests

Thick forests of giant redwoods create very special conditions along California's north coast. The wildflowers that bloom under the towering trees have adapted to the very moist and shady habitat. This unusual environment actually supports fewer wildflowers than mountain meadows, deserts, or other types of forests. Look for these gorgeous wildflowers in the deep redwood forests of northern California.

Trillium

other names: Wake Robin
height: 4" to 16"
season: February to June

Tri in the word trillium means three. This striking flower has three large leaves and three white petals which turn pink to reddish with age. Trillium has the common name Wake Robin because it blooms early in the spring—about the time the first robins arrive. Ants love the trillium's oil-rich seeds and help scatter them throughout the forest. If you pick the bloom from a trillium the plant may die or may not bloom again for years. Take a picture—it will last longer!

Yellow Violet

other names: Stream Violet, Pioneer Violet
height: 2" to 12"
season: March to July

How can a violet be yellow instead of purple? Violets actually come in many colors. There are over 300 species in the world. The yellow violet has heart-shaped leaves and five yellow petals. The lower, larger petal forms a landing platform for bees, which are attracted to the color yellow. Even purple violets have yellow in their throats to attract bees.

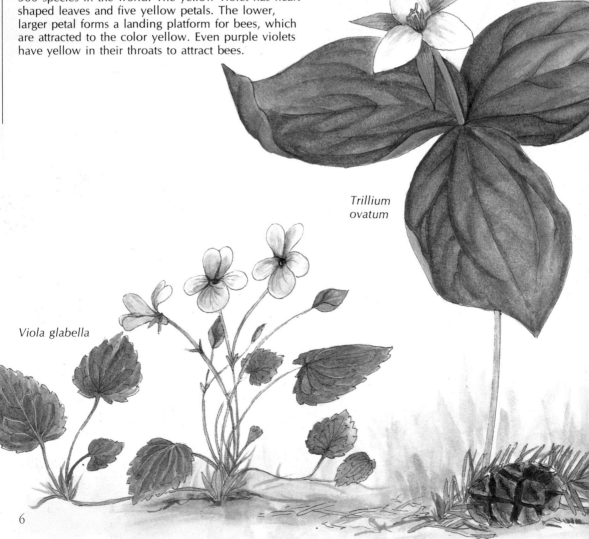

Trillium ovatum

Viola glabella

Tiger Lily

other names: Columbia Lily,
    Turk's Cap, Leopard Lily
height: 2' to 7'
season: May to August

These bright orange blossoms with purplish spots are easy to recognize. They are the color of a tiger or leopard! The petals and sepals curve away from the long slender stamens. Leaves grow in whorls of 10-20, and form tiers along the stem.

Douglas' Iris

other names: Blue Flag,
    Mountain Iris
height: 6" to 30"
season: March to May

Iris is Greek for rainbow. If you look into the center of the petals you will see a rainbow of colors. Iris grow in crowds and many types are found around the world. In fact, one iris, the fleur-de-lis or Flower of Louis was adopted by King Louis VII as the emblem of France. Native Americans used the silky fibers from the leaves to make twine and rope for fishing and hunting.

Redwood Sorrel

other names: Sour Grass, Sour
    Clover, Oxalis, Shamrock,
    Wood Sorrel
height: 2" to 12"
season: April to September

Redwood sorrel is often so abundant that it carpets the forest floor. Oxalis comes from the Greek word for sour and the tart juice of the leaves has a pleasant taste. Some people use them in salads. Redwood sorrel has tiny white or pink flowers, and heart-shaped, clover-like leaves.

Oxalis oregana

...um humboldtii

Iris douglasiana

Chocolate Lily

other names: Mission Bells, Leopard
　　　　　Lily, Checker Lily
height: 1' to 4'
season: February to June

Such an unusual color! The
deep purple petals, almost
chocolate in color, and sepals of
the bell-shaped blossom have
greenish-yellow polka dots and
stripes. The underground bulb
　　　　　was eaten by
　　　　　Native Americans.

Spring Beauty

other names: Indian Potato,
　　　　　Groundnut
height: 2'' to 10''
season: April to July

Look closely to notice the
thin pink lines and spot of
yellow decorating the flower.
Each of the five petals is
notched at the top. The nutty-
tasting corm, a thick underground base, was eaten by
Native Americans.

Yellow Bell

other names: Yellow Fritillary
height: 4'' to 12''
season: March to June

The dainty, yellow, bell-
shaped flower fades to
purplish with age, and narrow
grass-like leaves sprout on the
stem. *Pudica*, part of its
scientific name, means
bashful, as the drooping
flowers always hide their
faces. Bears, deer, and other
animals eat this plant.

Fritillaria pudica

Fritillaria lanceo

Claytonia lanceolata

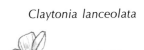

Coastal Forests

The ocean sends rain and fog onto the coast, where moisture-loving trees, shrubs, and flowers grow in abundance. Thick, tall oaks and yew trees mix with maple, alder, and dogwood. Bushes and shrubs grow in dense thickets that are difficult to walk through. It's a delight to come upon a lovely wildflower peeking out from the shelter of a towering tree.

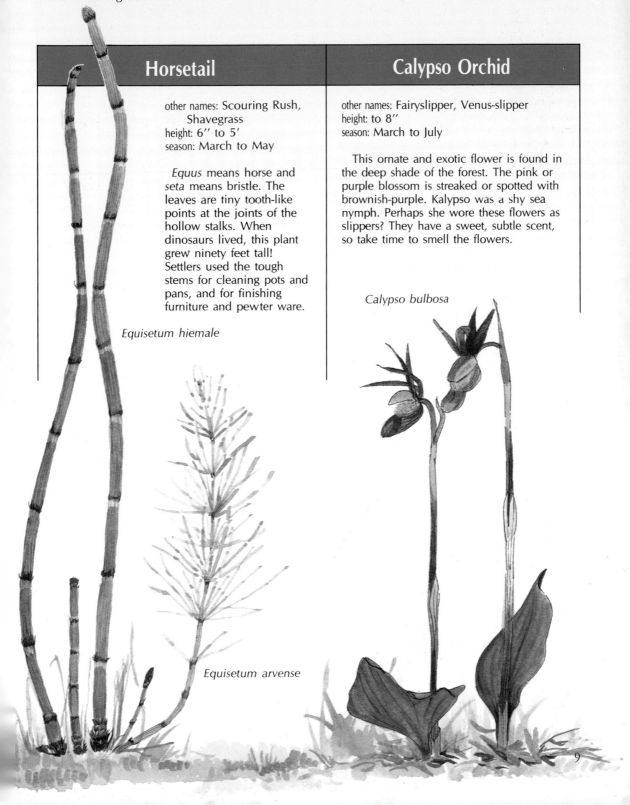

Horsetail

other names: Scouring Rush,
        Shavegrass
height: 6″ to 5′
season: March to May

 Equus means horse and *seta* means bristle. The leaves are tiny tooth-like points at the joints of the hollow stalks. When dinosaurs lived, this plant grew ninety feet tall! Settlers used the tough stems for cleaning pots and pans, and for finishing furniture and pewter ware.

Equisetum hiemale

Equisetum arvense

Calypso Orchid

other names: Fairyslipper, Venus-slipper
height: to 8″
season: March to July

 This ornate and exotic flower is found in the deep shade of the forest. The pink or purple blossom is streaked or spotted with brownish-purple. Kalypso was a shy sea nymph. Perhaps she wore these flowers as slippers? They have a sweet, subtle scent, so take time to smell the flowers.

Calypso bulbosa

Prince's Pine

other names: Pipsissewa
height: 2'' to 12''
season: June to August

A charming plant whose waxy hanging flowers resemble a pink crown. Native Americans used the leathery, dark green leaves as a remedy for kidney and bladder afflictions. The name Pipsissewa comes from the Cree Indian word "pipisisikwe," meaning "breaks into small pieces."

Indian Pipe

other names: Ghost Plant,
    Corpse Plant
height: 2'' to 12''
season: June to August

This waxy, translucent white flower droops atop its stalk, and resembles an Indian peace pipe. It will turn black if you touch it, or as it gets old. A fungus growing on its roots helps it get nutrients from neighboring green plants.

Snow Plant

other names: none
height: 8'' to 24''
season: April to July

Once you glimpse this bright red plant poking up through the snow, you'll never forget it. It is a saphrophyte and lives on decaying leaves and twigs. The closely-packed hanging flowers are bell-shaped, atop the crimson scaly stalk.

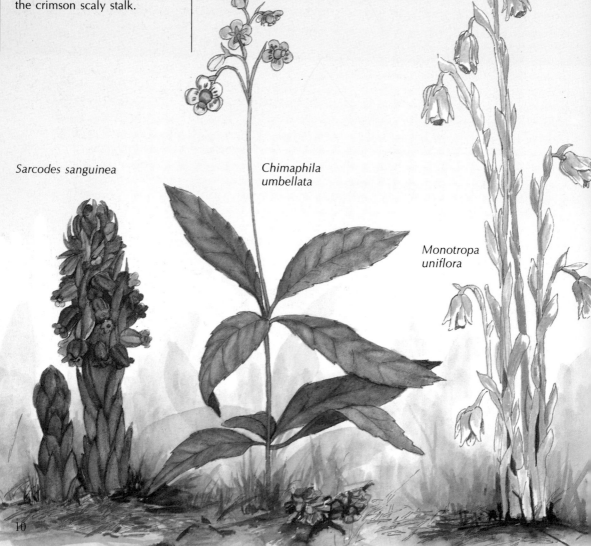

Sarcodes sanguinea

Chimaphila umbellata

Monotropa uniflora

Douglas-fir Forests

Douglas-fir remind us of Christmas trees. They make thick forests, often mixed with other kinds of fir and pine trees. Many shrubs and bushes grow along forest streams or in adjacent meadows. Chokecherry, huckleberry (yum!), and elderberry are some of the berries people love to pick from Douglas-fir forests. Some wildflowers like the cool shade of the deep woods while others grow in sunny clearings. Listen for an owl's hoot at night, and watch for chipmunks playing in the mornings.

Twinflower

other names: Linnaeus' Flower
height: 2'' to 4''
season: June to September

Two, drooping, bell-shaped flowers atop a single stem make this easy to identify. Linnaeus was one of the world's greatest naturalists. The scientific names we use today follow his method of classification.

Bunchberry

other names: Dwarf, Canadian, or Alaskan
  Dogwood, Puddingberry, Pigeonberry
height: 2'' to 8''
season: June to August

Four white petal-like bracts open around tiny greenish flowers in the center, which ripen into bright-red berries. The bland berries are eaten by birds, animals, and people.

Cornus canadensis

Linnaea borealis

11

Pine Forests

The Western Yellow Pine, also known as Ponderosa Pine, is a tall, straight tree with red-brown, grooved bark. It is very tolerant of dry arid regions and can grow on steep rocky soils. The long needles grow in clusters, letting sunlight filter down. The Yellow Pine forest floor is often quite open, with shrubs and plenty of grasses. Look for pretty pink wild roses and shiny green kinnikinnick as you meander about.

Shooting Stars

other names: Peacock Flower, Bird's Bill, Sailor Cap, Mosquito Bill
height: 4″ to 24″
season: April to August

There are approximately ten species of shooting stars in the West. Flower color ranges from white to pink to deep purple. They all share the appearance of being inside out—that is, of "shooting" downward. Native Americans roasted and ate the roots and leaves.

Ladyslipper Orchid

other names: California Ladys-slipper
height: 8″ to 20″
season: April to June

This breathtaking beauty has many sisters—Yellow Ladys-slipper, Sparrow's Egg Ladys-slipper, Mountain Ladys-slipper—all similar in size with the same odd shape. The lower petal forms a pouch, and the stamens and pistil make a column inside. "Cypri" is Greek for Venus, the goddess of love. Perhaps she is the lady who wore flowers for shoes?

Larkspur

other names: Delphinium
height: 4″ to 16″
season: March to July

If you use your imagination, this plant in profile resembles a bird's foot complete with a spur. The spur is really one of the five sepals. The sepals and petals range from blue or purple to white. There are many species of larkspurs from grasslands to mountain tops. It is poisonous to humans and cattle.

Delphinium nuttallianum

Cypripedium californicum

Dodecatheon pulchellum

Mariposa Tulip

other names: Mariposa Lily
height: 6" to 24"
season: April to June

Mariposa is Spanish for butterfly. You can easily imagine the petals as the delicate wings of a butterfly. This lily and its relatives grow in meadows, hillsides, and desert foothills. Colors range from white to blue, maroon, yellow, or orange-red. At the base of its three petals is a colored spot and a mat of fine hairs that aid in pollination. The small bulbs were baked and eaten by Native Americans, explorers and settlers.

Cranesbill

other names: Richardson's
   Geranium, Sticky
   Geranium, Stork's Bill
height: 8" to 32"
season: June to August

Look for the delicate pink- or purple-tinged veins in the white or pink petals. Geranium comes from the Greek word "geranos," meaning crane. The long-beaked seed pods that appear after the flower fades and falls resembles a crane's or stork's bill. Each style is attached to a seed and twists like a corkscrew to help the seeds separate and disperse.

*Geranium
richardsonii*

*Calochortus
luteus*

Monkeyflower

other names: Wild Lettuce
height: to 3'
season: March to September

The charming yellow flowers of this plant lift their laughing faces (*mimulus* means mimic) and smile at the passerby. Each flower has crimson spots on the lower lip accenting its smile. There are many different species of monkeyflower. They may be yellow, orange, red, or purple. Monkeyflowers grow in clusters, usually near streams. If the plant falls over, roots will develop where the stems touch soil. Native Americans and early settlers ate it raw or cooked.

*Mimulus
guttatus*

Blue Camas

other names: Quamash,
           Common Camas
height: 12″ to 20″
season: April to June

The Blue Camas is a nourishing food. Native Americans depended on it, and it was the main vegetable of many settlers' diets. The Chief Joseph War started when the Nez Perce Indians left their reservation to go south to collect camas for the coming winter.

Elephant Head

other names: Little Red Elephants
height: 6″ to 30″
season: June to August

On close examination of the flower stalk, it is easy to see how this one got its name. With its trunk raised in trumpeting and ear-like petals to either side, this flower only needs eyes to resemble a real pink elephant.

Explorer's Gentian

other names: Mountain
           Gentian
height: 2″ to 12″
season: July to October

One of the loveliest mountain meadow flowers, this vase-shaped bloom can be found throughout the West. The blossoms open in the morning and close for the cool nights. The roots of the gentian were prepared as a tea by Native Americans and settlers to treat indigestion and other distresses.

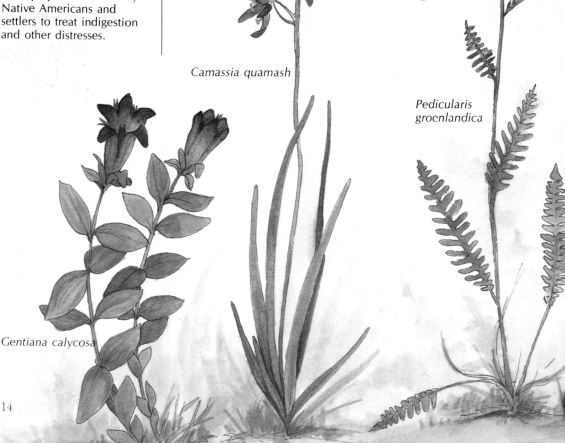

Camassia quamash

Pedicularis groenlandica

Gentiana calycosa

14

Mountain Meadows

Mountain meadows lie under snow much of the winter, are awash with water in the spring and early summer, and often dry out completely in late summer and autumn. Plants must be able to blossom quickly and then wait patiently until the next summer warms them again.

Corn Lily

other names: California Corn Lily, False Hellebore
height: 3' to 8'
season: June to August

From a distance the tall stalk and deeply veined leaves of this plant make it look like garden corn. Virtually all parts of this plant are poisonous. Cattle and humans have suffered from eating this plant.

Western Columbine

other names: Red Columbine
height: 12'' to 3'
season: April to August

The unique shape and color of this five petaled nodding flower make it easy to distinguish. Its scientific name *Aquilegia formosa* means "beautiful eagle" and refers to its trailing tubular petals which resemble eagle talons. These petals are so long only long-tongued insects or long-beaked birds (like hummingbirds) can pollinate them. Bumble bees will cut holes in the spurs to get at the nectar.

Veratrum californicum

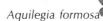

Aquilegia formosa

15

Cattail

other names: Bullrush
height: 4' to 8'
season: June to November

Standing in shallow water, this plant waves its brown cat-like tail. Many waterfowl and shorebirds depend on it for nesting habitat. Indians used the leaves for weaving, the downy seeds for insulation and padding, the pollen for flour, and the flowers and roots for food.

Typha latifolia

Skunk Cabbage

other names: none
height: 1' to 2'
season: April to July

The common name refers to the skunk-like odor of this plant. Bears and other animals love to eat the peppery-tasting roots. The 6" - 12" yellow spike that appears inside a yellow cloak is actually the flower. The leaves can grow up to five feet long.

Indian Pond Lily

other names: Spatterdock,
    Yellow Water Lily, Wokas
height: 1' to 3'
season: April to September

The heart-shaped, leathery, large (4" to 18") leaves often float on the water, holding up the waxy, cup-shaped yellow flower. Underwater, the sinewy roots wind into an eerie labyrinth of tangles and webs. The seeds were roasted on top of a fire like popcorn or ground into flour by Native Americans.

Marsh Marigold

other names: Twin Flower,
    Cowslip, Anemone
height: 2" to 6"
season: April to July

This water-loving plant is found near receding snowbanks or next to streams and lakes. The kidney-shaped leaves are bright green, often with purple veins on the undersides. The blossom has no petals but its five to twelve sepals look like white petals.

Caltha howellii

Nuphar polysepalum

Lysichiton ame

Marsh, Pond, & Wetland Plants

Sploosh! Splash! You have to get your feet wet to see some flowers. Many plants need so much water that they grow with their roots entirely submerged. Brightly-colored flowers bloom alongside a lake, right next to a melting snowfield, or in a boggy field. They live in the company of beavers, otters, and the many animals who come to the water to drink.

Pitcher Plant

other names: Cobra Plant, Cobra Lily
height: to 3'
season: April to August

This plant actually eats insects! It attracts them by secreting a sweet nectar in its cobra-like hood and mustache-like appendages. Insects attracted to the smell enter the hole in the underside of the hood. As they try to escape, hair-like barbs keep them from flying away. They can only move downward toward their doom. Fluid in the base of this plant helps decompose and eventually digest the trapped and unlucky insect.

Darlingtonia Californica

Roundleaf Sundew

other names: none
height: to 10"
season: June to September

The name refers to tiny dew-like drops of sticky fluid found on the leaf hairs. Insects attracted to these bright red tentacles stick to the dew and are eventually digested by the plant. Sundews need minerals not supplied by the boggy earth in which they grow and have evolved the ability to digest the fleshy parts of insects.

Drosera rotundifolia

17

Desert Aster

other names: Mojave Aster
height: 1' to 2'
season: March to May and
again in October

Each lavender blossom is a
flowerhead. The ''petals'' are
actually dozens of ray-flowers, and
the center disk is composed of
many tiny flowers. This widely
branched plant resembles other
asters found in fields and meadows.

Desert Lily

other names: Ajo (AH-hoe)
height: 1' to 6'
season: March to May

The onion-like bulb grows
one to two feet beneath the
desert surface, and was eaten
by Papago Indians. The leaves
have wavy edges and the
fragrant, fragile blossom has a
trumpet-like shape. It opens
in the day to greet the sun,
and closes each night.

*Hesperocallis
undulata*

*Machaeranthera
tortifolia*

Sand Verbena

other names: none
height: stems trail
up to 2' long
season: March to
October

During a wet
spring this plant
carpets miles of
desert with soft pink or purple
blossoms. The flowers grow in
clusters atop the thick, hairy
leaves and sticky stems. One
whiff of the fragrance
and you'll come
back for more.

Abronia villosa

Desert Flowers

When we think of the desert, we think of rock and sand and perhaps a lone cactus. But despite harsh and variable conditions, the desert hosts delicate wildflowers and succulent cacti, spiny shrubs and hardy trees. These plants have adapted in many ways and show off their colorful finery at different times of the year.

Many desert flowers are annuals, growing each year from a seed into a beautiful flower in just a few weeks. Rather than trying to endure the blistering heat or freezing cold of the desert seasons, they let their tough seeds await a gentle rain. Sometimes they have to wait several years before conditions are right. Then they quickly germinate, grow, blossom, and produce more seeds.

Cacti are perennials. That is, they live more than two years, so they must be experts at enduring the desert's dry heat. They have evolved specialized parts which store water through dry seasons. Different species of cacti bloom during much of the year. It is a real treat to see their brilliant, jewel-like blossoms which usually last only a few hours.

Ghost Flower

other names: Mojave Flower
height: 4" to 20"
season: March to April

Seemingly too delicate for the harsh desert sun, the translucent blooms of this yellow flower decorate rocky slopes and desert washes. The ghostly pale petals spotted with maroon freckles give this cup-shaped flower give its name "Ghost Flower."

Birdcage Evening Primrose

other names: Desert Primrose
height: 2" to 12"
season: March to May

Insects flying at night are attracted to this thin white flower which opens in late afternoon. The blossom turns pink as it wilts in the next day's bright sun. When the plant dies, the stems curve upward, forming a "birdcage."

Oenothera deltoides

Mohavea confertiflora

Cactus

Hundreds of species of cacti grow in California, on high mountains, along the seashore, and on grassy plains. They also, of course, grow where we most often think of them—in the desert.

Cacti—those spiny, odd-shaped plants—produce beautiful, brightly colored blossoms. Botanists believe cactus are related to carnations.

A cactus sends down a tap root to anchor the plant in the ground. Shallow roots spread around the tap root like an umbrella. These roots suck up moisture from even small rain showers. The cactus changes the water into a thick substance which does not evaporate quickly and stores it in expandable tissues. When plenty of rain falls, many cacti swell up with

Teddy Bear Cholla

other names: Tesajo, Jumping Cactus
height: 2' to 4'
season: May to September

This is not the kind of teddy bear to cuddle! Although it looks soft and fuzzy, tiny barbs on the end of each spine stick in your skin at the slightest touch. New plants form when joints from the plant drop onto the ground and take root. The pretty flowers are greenish-yellow, often streaked with lavender.

Opuntia bigelovii

Prickly Pear & Beavertail

other names: none
height: to 5'
season: April to July

These are the best-known cacti throughout the West. The pear-shaped fruits are eaten by animals and people. Flattened pods, or stem joints, resemble a beaver's tail. The yellow blossoms are gorgeous and often cover the entire plant.

Opuntia basilaris

Opuntia mojavensis

the feast and then very slowly use that stored water to help them through dry spells. Some cacti survive on stored fluids for several years.

Spines on cacti grow in bunches from common centers. Thick, waxy skin hinders evaporation of precious fluids, and food is manufactured by the outer green cells of the stems. All cactus fruit is edible and tastes good!

Barrel Cactus

other names: Devil's Head, Bisnaga, Compass Cactus
height: to 10''
season: March to May

Accordion-like pleats swell up with water, enabling this plant to live for years just on stored fluids. Cells grow faster on the shaded side, so this cactus often "points" toward the sunny south, hence the name compass cactus. The spines are stout and grow in clusters, almost hiding the green skin. Pretty flowers are yellow or reddish, and the stem tissue is used to make cactus candy.

Ferocactus acanthodes

Hedgehog Cactus

other names: Strawberry Cactus, Claret Cup
height: 2'' to 12''
season: April to June

Bright scarlet flowers produce strawberry-red fruits which are sweet and juicy. The plant grows in clumps, and the fruit is very important in the diet of birds and rodents. Some species have rows of colorful spines.

Echinocereus triglochidiatus

Fishhook Cactus

other names: Pincushion, Button Cactus
height: to 10''
season: April to June

Pink or lavender flowers decorate this low-growing, clumpy cactus. The long spine in the center of a cluster of spines is curved at the tip like a fishhook. Don't let it catch you!

Mamillaria microcarpa

Oak Forests

Rolling foothills are often dotted with blue oak and digger pine trees. Grasses cover the ground, and it's easy to run and jump as you scout around for wildflowers.

Miner's Lettuce

other names: Indian Lettuce,
      Squaw Cabbage
height: 1″ to 14″
season: March to July

A bright-green bowl of leaves cradles a bouquet of tiny pinkish-white flowers. The juicy leaves and stems were eaten by Native Americans and early settlers.

Fairy Lantern

other names: White Glove-
      flower, Snowdrops,
      Satin Bells, Indian
      Bells, Globe Lily
height: 6″ to 30″
season: April to June

Satiny white blossoms and nodding, pale green buds hang like lanterns in the forest. The seed capsule develops into a lovely barely-green fruit.

Indian Pink

other names: none
height: 6″ to 36″
season: March to September

The brilliant, crimson, pinwheel-like petals have fringed edges. Below the soft, downy leaves a taproot goes deep in the ground in search of water.

Silene californica

Calochortus albus

Montia perfoliata

Blue-eyed Grass

other names: Grass Widow
height: 4″ to 20″
season: February to September

Six blue-violet petals form a star around a bright yellow "eye" in the center. The leaves are slender and grass-like, the stem flattened.

Sisyrinchium bellum

Chinese Houses

other names: Innocence
height: 1′ to 2′
season: March to June

With a fairyland appearance, these delicate purple flowers look like tiny pagodas, or many-storied Chinese buildings. Flowers form tiers of perfect circles around a single stem.

Collinsia heterophylla

Farewell to Spring

other names: Summer's Darling, Herald of Summer, Godetia
height: 6″ to 36″
season: June to August

Look for a dark red or purple spot on each petal. The showy pink, lavender, or purple flowers open each morning in late spring, when the green grassy slopes begin to turn golden in the summer sun.

Clarkia amoena

23

Queen Ann's Lace

other names: Wild Carrot
height: 1' to 4'
season: May to September

Flat-topped, lacy, white flowers cluster around a single, dark purple center flower. This is the ancestor of today's garden carrot. It is so pretty that in the 1700s an English queen wore it instead of real lace.

Milk Thistle

other names: none
height: 3' to 6'
season: May to July

The giant prickly leaves, lined with milky veins and spotted white, can grow to eighteen inches long and twelve inches wide. The reddish-purple flower heads are surrounded by a thick covering of short, curved thorns. Butterflies and honeybees love the blooms, and birds eat the seeds.

Fireweed

other names: Willowherb, Blooming Sally
height: 2' to 6'
season: June to September

This hardy plant is one of the first plants to grow after a fire or disturbance of the soil. The rose or lilac flowers turn into seeds which have long tufts of silky hair. These can be carried long distances by the wind. The tough fibrous stems were made into twine and rope by Native Americans.

Epilobium angustifolium

Silybum marianum

Daucus carota

24

A fire, bulldozer, or vehicle can tear up and destroy the ground in some places. Some plants, often thought of as weeds, are able to grow on these disturbed areas. They are an important part of nature because they stabilize the soil with their roots, add needed nutrients, and prepare the way for grasses, shrubs, and trees to grow there again. Next time you see a giant thistle growing alongside the road, remember its essential role in bringing back more plant life to the area.

California Poppy

other names: none
height: 6''to 24''
season: February to November

The grayish-green, fern-like leaves support the bright orange or yellow flowers which open on sunny, bright days. It is so widespread that whole hillsides are sometimes covered with the blossoms. This is the state flower of California and is now protected by law.

Eschscholtzia californica

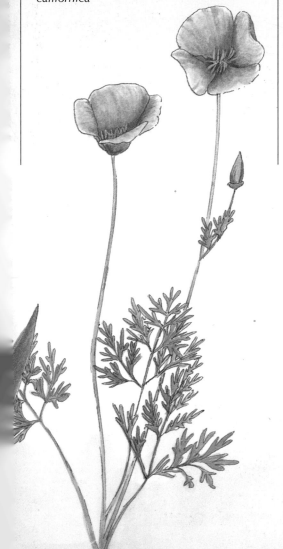

Lupine

other names: Bluebonnet
height: 8'' to 30''
season: April to May

Lupine means wolf, and early people named this flower the "wolf" because they mistakenly believed it robbed nutrients from the soil. In fact, it can only grow on poor soil, and its special nitrogen-stabilizing bacteria actually help enrich the soil. Lupine comes in many colors and sizes, and grows from the deserts to the mountaintops.

Lupinus spp.

Mushrooms

What curious-looking things mushrooms are! Some are as tiny as a grain of salt while others grow to be giants several feet wide. There are over 38,000 kinds of mushrooms in the world, with shapes that range from the traditional "toadstool" to others that look like a little bird's nest or a piece of underwater coral. Some cast a soft light, others have odors that are like fruit or licorice—or stinky. Colors vary from emerald green to scarlet, indigo blue to pale yellow, with many shades of brown and grey earth tones, too. Mushrooms are part of a family called fungi. Fungi are an important part of our world. The only place they cannot live is where there is no other life. Since they cannot produce chlorophyll, they must get nourishment from other life.

Puffball

other names: Western
      Giant Puffball
size: 3" to 36"
season: after heavy spring or
      summer rains

Young puffballs are white, with a fleshy, sometimes warty surface. When mature they turn brown. Spores inside the ball are released in a *poof!* when the mature puffball is touched. The patter of a raindrop is enough pressure for the puffball to shoot out its spores. It has been calculated that an average everyday puffball contains seven trillion spores. Puffballs can weigh up to four pounds, and have been mistaken for skulls lying in a field, hence the French name Tête de Mort.

Morel

other names: Sponge Morel
height: to 6"
season: spring

This delicious mushroom is a favorite of many people. It often grows among pine cones in the company of Calypso Orchids. The deeply honeycombed surface makes a morel easy to recognize. Yet, it has a poisonous look-a-like known as the "False Morrel."

Chanterelle

other names: Golden Chanterelle,
      Pfifferling
height: to 3"
season: autumn through winter
      and spring

The chanterelle is a funnel-shaped, golden mushroom with wavy, curled edges on its cap. It smells like dried peaches or pumpkins. The taste is mild or peppery, and delicious. Look for it under Douglas-fir or oak trees.

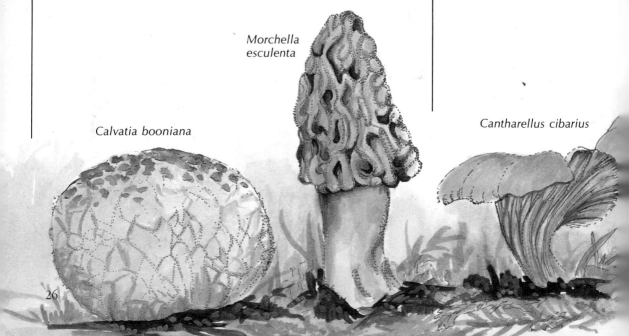

Morchella esculenta

Calvatia booniana

Cantharellus cibarius

Fungi play a primary role in decomposition. Think what the world would look like if nothing decomposed . . . the forests would be choked with dead plants and trees piled miles high. As the fungi absorb nutrients from dead or dying plants, they release carbon dioxide, minerals and other nutrients which other plants use as they grow.

The part we see and call a mushroom is actually the fruit of the plant. Much of a mushroom's life goes on underground, sometimes for years, before it sends its fruit above ground. A mushroom spore is like a green plant's seed. If the spore lands in a suitable place, it grows mycelium, which are delicate cobweb-like threads. The mycelium are like the roots, stem and leaves of green plants. This feathery network grows entirely underground, or inside trees. When ready, the mycelium sends out its fruit which grows very rapidly and produces spores. The spores are so tiny you need a magnifying glass to see one. Millions of them together make a very fine powdery-looking pile. Scientists have estimated that one average mushroom can produce 16 billion spores! Mushrooms release their spores in different ways. Some simply let them drop out, others wait for insects to carry them off, and one kind has a sort of catapult system which launches them! Many mushrooms are edible, but some are poisonous. Never eat a mushroom unless you can identify it positively and know it is safe. It is far better to simply enjoy watching them grow.

Fly Mushroom

other names: Fly Agaric
height: 2″ to 10″
season: spring and autumn

The brilliant red cap with white spots fades to an orange-yellow color with age. This is the pretty mushroom printed on dishtowels and stationery, or drawn by artists for fairies and gnomes to sit on. Find it under aspens or conifers, but don't eat this poisonous mushroom. Its name comes from the historic practice of mixing its fleshy cap with milk to draw and poison house flies.

Coral Mushroom

other names: none
height: 3″ to 6″
season: late summer into autumn

It's not hard to imagine this rusty-yellow or pink fungus as an underwater coral, swaying in the tropical ocean currents. The many branches hold the spores at their tips. It grows in the cool, moist ground under conifers.

Ramaria botrytis

Amanita muscaria

Conclusion

The bright colors, attractive shapes, and sweet smells of wildflowers invite us to touch and learn. They provide an easy and enjoyable introduction to the natural world.

All of nature is interconnected. We humans are as dependent on clean air and water as is the tiniest wildflower. Next time you stoop down to inhale a flower's rich fragrance, remember that we, too, blossom and unfold in the natural world. Learn all you can and treat it gently—the earth is our most precious treasure.

*"The first rule of intelligent tinkering
is to save all the pieces."*

Aldo Leopold,
Sand County Almanac

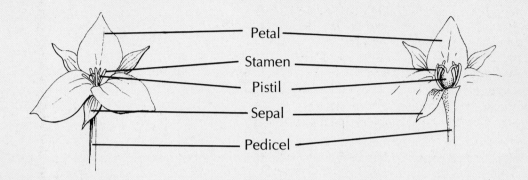

Petal
Stamen
Pistil
Sepal
Pedicel

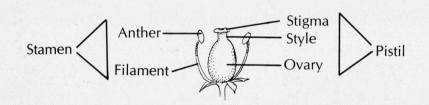

Stamen
Anther
Filament
Stigma
Style
Ovary
Pistil

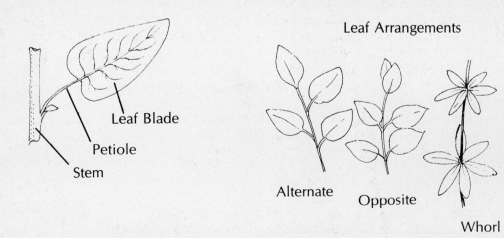

Leaf Blade
Petiole
Stem

Leaf Arrangements

Alternate
Opposite
Whorl

Glossary

Alpine	Pertaining to or inhabiting mountains.
Alternate	Not opposite each other.
Annual	A plant that lives for one season.
Anther	The part of the stamen containing pollen.
Berry	A fleshy fruit containing seeds.
Biennial	A plant that lives for two years.
Bulb	A plant bud usually below the ground.
Corm	A bulb-like underground swelling of a stem.
Composite	Flower heads composed of clusters of ray and disk flowers.
Disk flower	The tubular flowers in the center part of a composite flower head.
Evergreen	Bearing green leaves throughout the year.
Filament	The stalk of the stamen.
Flower head	A dense cluster of flowers atop a stem.
Fruit	Seed-bearing part of a plant; ripened ovary.
Fungus	A plant lacking chlorophyll which reproduces by spores.
Gland	A spot or area that produces a sticky substance.
Habitat	The community where a plant naturally grows and lives.
Head	A dense cluster of flowers atop a stem.
Herb	A plant with no woody stem above ground.
Hybrid	A cross between two species.
Irregular	Nonsymmetrical in shape.
Nectar	A sweet liquid produced by flowers that attracts insects.
Opposite	Pairs of leaves opposite each other on a stem.
Ovary	Part of the pistil which contains the developing seeds.
Parasitic	Growing on and deriving nourishment from another plant.
Pedicel	The supporting stem of a single flower.
Perennial	A plant that lives from year to year.
Petals	The floral leaves inside the sepals which attract pollinators.
Petiole	The stem supporting a leaf.
Pistil	The seed-bearing organ of a flower.
Pollen	Powder-like cells produced by stamens.
Ray flower	The flowers around the edge of a flower head; each flower may resemble a single petal.
Regular	Alike in size and shape.
Rhizome	An underground stem or rootstock.
Saprophyte	A plant that lives on dead organic matter.
Sepal	Outermost floral leaf which protects the delicate petals.
Spur	A hollow appendage of a petal or sepal.
Stamen	The pollen producing organ of a flower.
Stigma	The end of the pistil that collects pollen.
Style	The slender stalk of a pistil.
Succulent	Pulpy, soft, and juicy.
Tendril	A slender twining extension of a leaf or stem.
Tuber	A thickened underground stem, having numerous buds.
Whorl	Three or more leaves or branches growing from a common point.

Interpreting the Great Outdoors

Nature's wonders, such as the wildflowers, are certainly remarkable, but unfortunately many people—especially young people—know little about them. That's one reason Falcon Press has launched this series of books called Interpreting the Great Outdoors.

Natural phenomena almost always have interesting and exciting stories behind them, stories too good to leave to scientists and naturalists. With this series of books, we hope to tell why, when, where, and how the wonders of nature came to be. We want to help satisfy the natural curiosity of our young readers.

Look for other books in Falcon Press' Interpreting the Great Outdoors series. They include *The Tree Giants: the story of the redwoods, the world's largest trees; The Fire Mountains: the story of the Cascade Volcanoes;* and *Where Dinosaurs Still Live.*

To obtain extra copies of this book or others in the Interpreting the Great Outdoors series, write to Falcon Press, P.O. Box 1718, Helena, MT 59624. Or call toll-free 1-800-582-BOOK. Falcon Press publishes and distributes a wide variety of books and calendars, so ask for our free catalog.